Poems of Osip Mandelstam

NEW DIRECTIONS POETRY PAMPHLETS

#1 Susan Howe: *Sorting Facts; or, Nineteen Ways of Looking at Marker*

#2 Lydia Davis / Eliot Weinberger: *Two American Scenes*

#3 Bernadette Mayer: *The Helens of Troy, NY*

#4 Sylvia Legris: *Pneumatic Antiphonal*

#5 Nathaniel Tarn: *The Beautiful Contradictions*

#6 Alejandra Pizarnik: *A Musical Hell*

#7 H.D.: *Vale Ave*

#8 Forrest Gander: *Eiko & Koma*

#9 Lawrence Ferlinghetti: *Blasts Cries Laughter*

#10 Osama Alomar: *Fullblood Arabian*

#11 Oliverio Girondo: *Poems to Read on a Streetcar*

#12 *Fifteen Iraqi Poets* (ed., Dunya Mikhail)

#13 Anne Carson: *The Albertine Workout*

#14 Li Shangyin: *Derangements of My Contemporaries*

#15 Sakutarō Hagiwara: *The Iceland*

#16 *Poems of Osip Mandelstam* (ed., Peter France)

Poems of Osip Mandelstam

SELECTED AND TRANSLATED FROM THE RUSSIAN BY
Peter France

NEW DIRECTIONS POETRY PAMPHLET #16

Earlier versions of some of these translations have appeared in the journals *Modern Poetry in Translation* and *Cardinal Points* (online version), and in *High on the Downs: A Festchrift for Harry Guest*, edited by Tony Lopez (Shearsman Books, 2012) and *Poets of Modern Russia* by Peter France (Cambridge University Press, 1983).

Cover design by Office of Paul Sahre
Interior design by Eileen Baumgartner and Erik Rieselbach
Manufactured in the United States of America
New Directions Books are printed on acid-free paper.
First published as New Directions Poetry Pamphlet #16 in 2014

Library of Congress Cataloging-in-Publication Data
Mandel'shtam, Osip, 1891–1938, author.
[Poems. Selections. English. 2014. Peter France]
Poems of Osip Mandelstam / translated from the Russian by Peter France.
pages ; cm—(New Directions poetry pamphlet ; #16)
ISBN 978-0-8112-2290-7 (alk. paper)
I. France, Peter, 1935– translator. II. Title.
III. Series: New Directions poetry pamphlets ; #16.
PG3476.M355A2 2014
891.71'3—dc23   201305000910

9 8 7 6 5 4 3 2 1

ndbooks.com

New Directions Books are published for James Laughlin
by New Directions Publishing Corporation
80 Eighth Avenue, New York 10011

Contents

Foreword   9

from **Stone** (1913/1916)

"Stretching tight the silken threads"   13
"Keen hearing stretches out a sail"   13
Silentium   14
"No, not the moon, a brightly lit clockface"   15
"I hate the steady gleam"   16
Notre Dame   17
The Admiralty   18
"Orioles in the woods—the length of vowels"   19
"Sleeplessness. Homer. Sails stretched tight"   19
"I shall not see the celebrated *Phèdre*"   20

from **Tristia** (1922)

"—How the splendor of these veils and this adornment"   22
"Cold chills my body. The transparent spring"   23
"In a deep sleigh, with straw spread for a litter"   24
"The thread of golden honey flowed from the bottle"   25
Freedom's Twilight   26
Tristia   27
"Heaviness, tenderness—sisters—your marks are the same"   28
"When Psyche-life, following Persephone"   29

"I have forgotten the word I wanted to say"   30
"Take from my palms some sun to bring you joy"   31
"Among the round of shades treading the tender meadow"   32
"Because I hadn't the strength to hold on to your hands"   33

from *Poems* (1928)

"I was washing at night out in the yard"   34
The Age   35
One Who Finds a Horseshoe (a Pindaric Fragment)   36
Slate Pencil Ode   40
January 1, 1924   43
"I shall fling myself through the dark streets'
    gypsy encampment"   46

Uncollected Poems (1930–1933)

Leningrad   47
"With imperial power I was only acquainted in childhood"   48
"Help me, O Lord, to live through this long night"   49
"We'll sit in the kitchen, you and I"   49
"For the noisy valor of future years"   50
Batyushkov   51
Ariosto   52

from the *Voronezh Notebooks* (1935–1937)

"I have to live, though twice now I have died"   54
Black Earth   55
"What's the name of this street?"   56
Children's Haircut   56
"Yes, lying in the earth, my lips are moving"   57
The Kama River   58
"Robbing me of the seas, a springboard and a sky"   59
"A wave runs on, wave breaking a wave's back"   59
"From past the houses and the trees"   60
"My goldfinch, I'll toss back my head"   60
"Deep in the hill the idol sits unmoving"   61
"Through my cabin windowpane"   62
"Day is a kind of greenhorn now"   62
"I'll marvel at the world, the snows"   63
"Yeast of the world, dear yeast of time"   63
"Alone, I look into the frost's face"   64
"What can we do with the deadness of the plains"   64
"I've not died yet, and still I'm not alone"   65
"Do not compare: life is incomparable"   66
"I hear the January ice"   66
"Like Rembrandt, martyr of the chiaroscuro"   67
"Armed with the eyesight of thin-waisted wasps"   68
"I sing when my throat is moist and my soul is dry"   68
"Rendings of rounded bays, and gravel, and deep blueness"   69
"O how I wish that I"   70
"The potters exalt the blue island"   71
"There are women who are akin to the damp earth"   72

Foreword

A great deal has been written about Mandelstam. Here I want to give just a brief chronological framework that may help readers see how his poetry is situated in a formidable and ultimately tragic life experience.

Osip Emilievich Mandelstam was born in Warsaw in 1891, the son of a leather merchant. He grew up in a Jewish milieu in St. Petersburg, where he attended school and university (in the Faculty of History and Philology). Much of the period between 1907 and 1910 was spent as a student in western Europe (France, Germany, Italy). In the years before the 1917 Revolution he was a member, with Nikolay Gumilev and Anna Akhmatova, of the Acmeist poets, who stood for clarity, this-worldliness, and the constructive principle, as against the mystical uncertainties of Symbolists. Later, Mandelstam was to define Acmeism as "nostalgia for world culture," and his poems refer constantly to the Greek, Roman, Italian, and French classics.

His first book bore the very Acmeist title *Stone*; first published in 1913, it received a second, expanded edition in 1916. The very different collection that followed, *Tristia* (1922), contained richly allusive poems written in the dramatic years from 1916 to 1920, years of world war, revolution, and civil war. The Ovidian title speaks for a recurrent preoccupation with loss, separation, exile, but unlike many writers and intellectuals, Mandelstam did not emigrate. His attitude toward the new revolutionary order was to remain for many years tensely ambivalent; writing and publication became more difficult throughout the 1920s.

In 1922 he married Nadezhda Yakovlevna Khazina, who subsequently accompanied him into internal exile and devoted herself to

9

preserving his work after his death. Many years later, she published remarkable and moving memoirs of their life, *Hope Against Hope* (1971) and *Hope Abandoned* (1974). The Mandelstams led a nomadic life within the Soviet Union, where he was increasingly excluded from serious literary work. The last volume of his verse to be published in his lifetime was *Poems* of 1928, which express in often oblique, hermetic language a tragic vision of life in Soviet Russia.

After 1930, which appears to have been a turning point, he began writing poems again more freely—and more dangerously. A grotesquely satirical portrait of Stalin became known to the authorities in 1934, and Mandelstam was arrested and sentenced to internal exile, first to the remote town of Cherdyn, then to the southern city of Voronezh, where he spent more than three years and wrote the challenging short poems contained in the *Voronezh Notebooks*. It is remarkable to set these densely living, jagged, image-studded poems against the calmer, more statuesque work he had written twenty years earlier, in an utterly different world.

Having been allowed to return to Moscow, he was again arrested in May 1938, sentenced to five years hard labor for "counterrevolutionary activities," and sent to eastern Siberia, where he died in December 1938. Thereafter, for many years he was omitted from Soviet literary history; his later poems only survived thanks to the efforts of Nadezhda Mandelstam and her friends, who committed them to memory. His complete works began to be published in New York in the 1960s; by the end of the century he was officially recognized in Russia as one of the greatest Russian poets. As well as his poetry, he left a considerable body of remarkable prose writings, essays, and autobiographical pieces, including the illuminating "Conversation About Dante."

While translating and discussing other Russian poets over the years, I have always been conscious that Mandelstam was an outstanding figure, arguably *the* outstanding Russian poet of the twentieth century, deploying an extraordinary wealth of word and image in verse of haunting melodic power. There have been many fine translations into English, and for a long time I hesitated to add to their number. If I have overcome this hesitation, it is mainly thanks to the encouragement of a number of readers, among whom I should mention Robert Chandler, himself an eminent translator, and Jeffrey Yang, with whom I have enjoyed working at New Directions for some ten years now. My gratitude goes to both of them, and to other friends too numerous to mention here.

This is a personal selection from the poetry. I have tried to make it reasonably representative of different strands and periods in Mandelstam's work, focusing above all on the anguished searchings of *Tristia*, the three great tragic "odes" of 1923–1924, and the brilliant and fragmentary Voronezh poems. The translations are generally close, seeking to offer an equivalent, not only to the meaning, but to the shape, the rhythms, and the verbal density of the often enigmatic and usually untitled originals. With a few exceptions, Mandelstam's poems are richly rhymed; without emulating him in this, I have used a variety of full rhymes, slant rhymes, internal rhymes, alliteration, and assonance in attempting to re-create in English what its author called a poetry of the voice.

Peter France
EDINBURGH, MARCH 2014

from **STONE** (1913/1916)

*

Stretching tight the silken threads
on the iridescent shuttle,
now begin your lesson, supple
fingers, begin your magic spells!

Ebbing and flowing of the hands,
movements of monotony,
you exorcise without a doubt
a panic terror of the sun,

when the broad palm, blazing like
a seashell, for a time grows dim
as the pull of shadows draws it in,
then moves back into rosy fire!

1909

*

Keen hearing stretches out a sail,
emptiness fills the widening eyes,
and through the quietness swims by
the noiseless choir of midnight birds.

I am as poor as nature is,
I am as simple as the sky,
my freedom is as tenuous
as voices of the midnight birds.

I see the moon devoid of life,
the sky more deathly than a sheet;
your eerie and distempered world
is welcome to me, emptiness!

1910

Silentium

She has not yet been born, and still
she is both music and the word,
and therefore the inviolable
union of all that moves on earth.

The ocean's breasts breathe peacefully,
but like a mad thing, day is bright,
and the foam's pale lilac lies
within a troubled bowl of light.

So let my lips now make their own
the dumbness of the primal days
like a note that is crystalline
in its original purity!

Aphrodite, still be foam,
let words be music once again,
and heart for heart still suffer shame
with pristine life again made one!

1910

★

No, not the moon, a brightly lit clockface
shines down on me, and how am I to blame
for seeing the milky weakness of the stars?

And I can't stomach Batyushkov's conceit:
"What time is it?" they asked him here on earth,
and his reply was just: "Eternity."

1912

[Konstantin Batyushkov (1787–1855), poet, precursor of Russia's "golden age," author of "Tasso Dying." He collapsed into insanity in 1821 and wrote no further poetry. See "Batyushkov" below in Uncollected Poems.*]*

*

I hate the steady gleam
of the monotonous stars.
Welcome, my ancient dream—
arrow thrust of the tower!

Stone, spread yourself in lace,
become a spider's web:
with a fine needle pierce
the heavens' empty breast.

My turn too will come—
I sense the wings stretched taut,
but where then can I aim
the arrow of living thought?

Perhaps I'll use my road
and time, then come back here:
There—I could not love,
here—love is my fear.

1912

Notre Dame

Here, where a Roman judge once judged an alien people,
stands a basilica, fresh-minted, full of joy;
as Adam long ago stood tall and flexed his sinews,
its muscles ripple through the light crisscrossing vaults.

Outside its walls you feel the hidden calculation—
like a saddle girth the power of arches planned
to hold in check the ponderous mass of stone from crushing
the walls, and neutralize the vaults' wild battering ram.

An elemental maze, unfathomable forest,
the reasoned vertigo that fills the gothic soul,
the power of Egypt, the humility of Christians,
an oak next to a reed—under the plumb line's rule.

But fortress Notre Dame, as more attentively
I gazed and studied your impenetrable frame,
I thought more and more often: let the mass be stubborn,
I too shall shape it to magnificence one day.

1912

The Admiralty

In the northern capital a dusty poplar languishes,
a transparent dial is tangled in the leaves,
and in the dark greenery, frigate, acropolis,
it shines from afar, a brother to sea and sky.

An airy vessel, mast of touchiness,
a rule for those who follow where Peter trod,
it teaches: beauty's no whim of a demigod,
but the keen reckoning of a joiner's eye.

Mastery of four elements gladdens the heart,
but human freedom has set up a fifth.
Is not the dominance of space denied
by the chaste lines of this created ark?

Capricious jellyfish cling angrily,
like plows abandoned anchors lie and rust—
and lo, the bonds of three dimensions break
and universal seas are opened up.

1913

*

Orioles in the woods—the length of vowels
in tonic verses is the only measure.
But one day only in the year does nature
brim with duration like Homeric meter.

The day yawns wide as if in a caesura
with peace and long-drawn work from dawn to night;
in the fields bullocks, and a golden leisure
to draw from reeds the wealth of a full note.

1914

*

Sleeplessness. Homer. Sails stretched tight.
I've read half through the catalogue of ships—
that long processional of cranes in flight
which once rose skyward over Greece.

An arrowhead of cranes aimed at a foreign land—
a godlike foam adorns the heads of kings—
where are you flying? If there was no Helen,
what would Troy be to you, Achaean men?

The sea and Homer, all things move in love.
Which should I listen to? Homer now is silent,
and like an orator the black sea roars
and with a ponderous crash breaks on my pillow.

1915

I shall not see the celebrated *Phèdre*
in the old-fashioned many-storied theater
with its high smoke-blackened gallery
by the guttering candles' light.
And, indifferent to the actors' bustle
as they gather in their harvest of applause,
I shall not hear across the footlights,
winged with its double rhyme the line:

—How these vain veils have grown repugnant to me . . .

The theater of Racine! A mighty barrier
divides us from this other universe;
between that world and ours there lies a curtain
that troubles us with its deep folds.
Classical shawls fall from the shoulders,
molten with suffering the voice grows stronger,
and the word white-hot with indignation
is tempered by the flame of grief . . .

I am too late for Racine's high festival!

Again the decaying posters rustle,
faint smells of orange peel drift out,
and as from the lethargy of ages
my neighbor stirs and says to me:
—Exhausted by Melpomene, her madness,
in this life it is peace alone I long for;
let us go before the jackal audience
tears the Muses limb from limb!

O if some Greek could see our pastimes ...

1915

from **TRISTIA** (1922)

            ★

—How the splendor of these veils and this adornment
weighs on me in the midst of my dishonor!

—Rocky Troezen will see
a famous calamity,
the royal palace steps
will blush red with shame,
. . . .
. . . .
and for the lovesick mother
a black sun will rise.

—If only it was hate that boiled within my breast—
but see how the confession escaped me unawares.

—With a black flame Phaedra burns
in the brightness of day.
A funeral torch smokes
in the brightness of day.
Fear your mother, Hippolytus:
Phaedra—night—lies in wait for you
in the brightness of day.

—With my black love I have besmirched the sun . . .
. . . .

—We are afraid, we do not dare
help the king in his grief.
Wounded by Theseus,
night has fallen on him.
But we with a funeral dirge,
bringing home the dead,
will sing to rest the black sun
of wild unsleeping passion.

                                                    1916

[*The reference is to Racine's* Phèdre, *but also to Euripides's* Hippolytus.]

                    *

Cold chills my body. The transparent spring
decks out Petropolis in pale green down,
but Neva's water, like a jellyfish,
inspires a faint revulsion in my soul.
On the embankment of the northern river
dragonflies and metallic beetles hover,
the fireflies of motorcars flash by
and the gold pins of stars gleam in the sky,
but there is no star able to destroy
the heavy emerald of the moving sea.

                                                    1916

*

In a deep sleigh, with straw spread for a litter,
the fateful matting barely kept us dry
from Sparrow Hills to that familiar chapel
the day we rode through Moscow's immensity.

But kids are playing knucklebones in Uglich,
it smells of bread left cooling in the oven.
They drive me through the streets, my head uncovered,
and in the little church three candles burn.

Not three candles were burning, but three meetings,
and one of them was blessed by God alone,
there will not be a fourth, Rome is far distant,
and he has never felt a love for Rome.

The sleigh went bumping over the black potholes,
the crowds were coming home from a day out,
the skinny peasant men, the bitter women
stood at the gates, shifting from foot to foot.

Black flocks of birds darken the dripping distance,
the hands are manacled, swollen and raw,
they drive the young prince in, numb and unfeeling,
and they have set alight the yellow straw.

1916

[Uglich was the scene of the murder of the young prince Dmitry, Ivan the Terrible's son, in 1591—see Pushkin's Boris Godunov. The poem is addressed to Marina Tsvetaeva.]

★

The thread of golden honey flowed from the bottle
so heavy and slow that our hostess had time to declare:
Here in melancholy Tauris, where fate has brought us,
we are not bored at all—and glanced back over her shoulder.

On all side the rites of Bacchus, as if the world
held only watchmen and dogs, not a soul to be seen—
the days roll peacefully by like heavy barrels:
Away in the hut are voices, you can't hear or reply.

We drank tea, then went out to the huge brown garden,
dark blinds were down like lashes over the eyes,
we walked past the white columns to look at the vineyard
where the somnolent hills are coated in airy glass.

I said: The vines are alive like ancient battles,
where curly horsemen are fighting in curving order,
in stony Tauris the science of Hellas lives on—
and the noble rusty array of golden acres.

And in the white room quiet stands like a spinning wheel,
smells of vinegar, paint, and wine that is fresh from the cellar.
Remember, in that Greek house, the much loved wife—
not Helen, the other wife—how long she embroidered?

Golden fleece, O where are you now, golden fleece?
All the journey long the heavy sea waves were loud,
and leaving his ship, his sails worn out by the seas,
full of space and time, Odysseus came home.

1917

[Tauris—the Crimea.]

Freedom's Twilight

Let's honor freedom's twilight, brothers,
honor the mighty twilight year.
Beneath the seething nighttime waters
the leaden weight of nets is sunk.
Into the dull years of stagnation
you rise up, people, judge and sun.

Let's honor, too, the fateful burden
the people's leader, all in tears, accepts.
Honor the darkening load of power
in its unbearable dead weight.
Who has a heart, must hear your vessel,
time, as it sinks to the seabed.

We have bound fast the warlike legions
of swallows—and at once the sun
is no more to be seen, and nature,
living and moving, chirps its song.
Through nets—the obscure face of twilight—
no sun is seen, the earth sails on.

What of it, then, let us attempt it,
the great unwieldy turn of the wheel.
The earth sails on. Men, show your courage.
Plowing a furrow through the seas,
we shall remember in cold Lethe
we paid ten heavens for this earth.

MOSCOW, MAY 1918

Tristia

I have studied the science of farewells
in the bare-headed grief of night.
The oxen chewing and the long-drawn wait,
the last hour of the city watch.
I know the ritual of the cock-crow night
when, lifting their load of travelers' grief,
the tear-filled eyes peered beyond sight
and muses' song mixed with women's tears.

Who can tell, when the word "farewell" is spoken,
what kind of separation lies before us,
what is foretold by the cock's exclamation,
when a fire is lit on the acropolis,
and at the dawn of some new life,
while the ox chews lazily in the stall,
why the cock, the herald of new life,
flaps his wings high on the city wall.

I love the rituals of weaving:
the shuttle scurrying, the spindle's hum,
and look, like swan's down, running barefoot
Delia is flying out to greet us!
O what a threadbare life we lead,
how pitifully poor the words of joy!
All has been seen, all will be seen again,
only the moment of recognition is sweet.

So be it: a transparent figurine
is lying on a clean earthenware dish
like the skin of a squirrel stretched out flat,
a girl bends over the wax and stares.
It's not for us to guess Greek Erebus,
wax is for women what bronze is for men:
only in battle do we meet our fate,
they find their death in divination.

1918

[Tristia (Sorrows) *is the title of a collection of verse epistles by Ovid written*
in exile.]

★

Heaviness, tenderness—sisters—your marks are the same.
The wasps and the honeybees suck at the heavy rose.
Man dies, heat drains from the once warm sand,
and on a black bier they carry off yesterday's sun.

O you tender nets and you heavy honeycombs,
Easier to lift a stone than to speak your name!
Only one care is left to me in the world:
a care that is golden, to shed the burden of time.

I drink the mutinous air like some dark water.
Time is turned up by the plow, and the rose was earth.
Slowly they eddy, the heavy, the tender roses,
roses of heaviness, tenderness, twofold wreath.

KOKTEBEL, MARCH 1920

*

When Psyche-life, following Persephone,
goes down to the shades in the half-forgotten trees,
a blind swallow flings itself against her feet
with Stygian tenderness and a branch still green.

A host of shades run out to meet her flight,
greeting their new friend with a keening note,
and gaze at her, and wring their feeble hands,
uncomprehending, full of fearful hope.

One holds a mirror, one a perfume flask—
the soul is a woman, trifles warm her heart—
and the bare wood filters their dry complaints,
transparent voices, like a fine small rain.

And in tender confusion, at a loss,
the soul can't recognize the transparent oaks,
breathes on a glass, reluctantly pays out
the copper coin for the misted ferryboat.

1920

*

I have forgotten the word I wanted to say.
The blind swallow will return to the hall of shades
on clipped wings to sport with transparent ones.
In unconsciousness the song of night is sung.

No sound of birds. No flower on the immortelles.
Transparent the manes of horses of the night.
In the dry river floats an empty shell.
Unconscious the word where the grasshoppers cry.

And gradually it grows, like a temple or tent.
Suddenly it will play the mad Antigone,
or like a dead swallow throw itself at the feet
with Stygian tenderness, a branch of green.

O to bring back the shame of seeing fingers
and convex recognition's happiness!
I am so fearful of the Muses' keening,
of clangor, mist, and yawning emptiness.

But mortals have power to love and recognize,
for them sound too flows through the finger ends,
but I have forgotten what I want to say,
the bodiless thought will return to the hall of shades.

The transparent one still sings to no avail,
still swallow, Antigone, beloved girl ... —
but on the lips like black ice I feel
the memory of Stygian clangor burn.

NOVEMBER 1920

*

Take from my palms some sun to bring you joy
and take a little honey—so the bees
of cold Persephone commanded us.

No loosing of the boat that is not moored,
no hearing of the shadow shod in fur,
no overcoming fear in life's dense wood.

And kisses are all that's left us now,
kisses as hairy as the little bees
who perish if they fly out of the hive.

They rustle in transparent depths of night,
their home the thick woods on Taigetos's slopes,
their food is honeysuckle, mint, and time.

So for your joy receive my savage gift,
a dry and homely necklace of dead bees
that have transmuted honey into sun.

NOVEMBER 1920

*

Among the round of shades treading the tender meadow,
I came down here to dance, with a sonorous name,
but it all melted from me, just a shadow
of sound in my misted memory remained.

At first I placed the name with the seraphim
and kept my distance from the fragile body,
but just a few days gone, I merged with it
and lost myself in its beloved shadow.

And once again the tree sheds its wild apples,
and a secret image flashes on my sight,
and it blasphemes, curses itself, and swallows
the burning coals that we call jealousy.

But happiness rolls by, like a golden hoop,
following the dictates of an alien will,
and you go chasing after fragile spring,
plowing the air with outstretched arms, and still

all is arranged in such a way that we
are held forever in the enchanted round.
The supple hills of the immaculate earth
lie tightly folded in their swathing bands.

1920

*

Because I hadn't the strength to hold on to your hands,
because I abandoned lips that are salty and loving,
I must wait for the day to return to the high city's dark.
How I hate them, these ancient ramparts smelling of resin!

The men of Achaea in darkness are shaping a horse,
and into its sides their sharp-toothed saws gnaw fiercely.
There's no way the blood's dry patter can be allayed,
there's no name for you, no sound, no mask, and no molding.

How could I, dare I have thought that you would return?
And why, when the time had come, did I desert you?
The darkness is not yet scattered, the cock has not sung,
the red-hot ax has not bitten into the timber.

Pitch has oozed out of the walls like transparent tears,
and the city can feel its ribs, their wooden structure,
but blood has welled up in the stairways and stormed the town,
and three times the Achaeans have seen it, the dream of temptation.

Where is lovely Troy, the king's and the maidens' house?
Priam's lofty aviary will be brought to nothing.
And arrows are raining down, a dry shower of wood,
and other arrows spring up from the earth like nut twigs.

The sting of the final star without any pain is stilled,
and morning like a gray swallow will beat at the window,
and unhurried day, like an ox that wakes in the straw,
in the squares that are rough from too much sleep is stirring.

DECEMBER 1920

*

I was washing at night out in the yard—
the heavens glowing with rough stars.
A star-beam like salt upon an ax,
the water barrel brimful and cold.

A padlock makes the gate secure,
and conscience gives sternness to the earth—
hard to find a standard anywhere
purer than the truth of new-made cloth.

A star melts in the barrel like salt,
and the ice-cold water is blacker still,
death is more pure, disaster saltier,
and earth more truthful and more terrible.

1921

The Age

My age, my beast, where is the man
who can look into your eyes
and join together with his blood
the vertebrae of two centuries?
Blood the builder gushes out
of every earthly creature's throat.
The parasite can only shake
on the threshold of new days.

A creature, while it clings to life,
must carry its backbone to the grave;
the spine within, invisible,
is tossed and tumbled by the waves.
And the earth's still-infant age
seems the soft cartilage of a child;
they have brought the crown of life,
like a lamb to the sacrifice.

To tear the age from captivity,
to begin the world anew,
the sections of uneven days
must be welded with a flute.
It is the age rocking the wave
with the grief of humankind
and in the grass the adder breathes
to the age's measure of gold.

And the new buds will swell again,
the sprouts of green splash forth,
but it is smashed to bits, your spine,
my age, pathetic, beautiful.
And with a smile that makes no sense
you look behind you, cruel and weak,
as a once agile beast looks back
at the tracks of its own feet.

1923

One Who Finds a Horseshoe
(a Pindaric Fragment)

We look to the forest and say:
a forest of ships, of masts,
the rose-colored pine trees
free of shaggy growth to the top
should go groaning into the storm,
lonely pines
in the furious treeless air;
under the wind's salty heel the plumb line holds firm, made fast to
the dancing deck.
And the seafarer
in his unbridled thirst for space,
dragging over damp furrows a geometer's fragile tools,
measures the pull of earth's heart
against the sea's rough face.

And inhaling the odor
of resinous tears that seep through the vessel's boarding,
admiring the planks
jointed and shaped into bulkheads
not by that peaceable Bethlehem carpenter but by another—
the father of journeys, the friend of seamen—
we say:
they too stood on earth
that was rough as a donkey's backbone,
tops forgetting their roots
on a noble mountain ridge,
and they rustled in freshwater showers
vainly pleading to heaven to change their illustrious burden
for a pinch of salt.

Where to begin?
Everything is cracking and rocking.
The air is shaking with similes.
No word is better than the next,
the earth buzzing with metaphor
and the light two-wheelers
harnessed brightly to bird flocks dense from the effort
break apart as they race
with the snorting lords of the stadium.

Thrice beloved is the man with a name in his song;
a song when adorned with a name
lives longer than the rest—
marked out from her friends by a headband
that cures her of swooning and over-strong odors—
the closeness of man
or the scent of the hide of a powerful beast
or simply the essence of savory crushed in the palm.

The air can be dark as water, all that lives in it swims like a fish,
pushing wide with its fins the sphere
that is full and elastic, just warm—
crystal, where wheels move and horses rear up,
damp black earth of Neaera, tilled each night anew
with forks, tridents, mattocks, and plows.
The air is entangled, as dense as the earth—
you cannot get out, but it's hard to get in.

Like a green racket, a rustle runs through the trees;
children play at jacks with vertebrae of animals long dead.
Our age's fragile chronology is nearing an end.
Thank you for what was:
I myself was mistaken, lost my way, lost count.
The epoch rang like a golden ball,
empty, cast metal, supported by no one,
at every touch it replied "yes" or "no."
So a child replies:
"I'll give you an apple" or "I won't give you an apple."
And his face is molded on the voice that speaks those words.

The sound resounds though the cause of the sound has gone.
The horse lies in the dust and snorts in its foam,
but the sharp twist of its neck
still remembers the race with legs thrown wide—
not four,
but as many as the stones on the road
relayed in four shifts as
the blazing heat of the racer pushes from earth.

So
one who finds a horseshoe
blows the dust from it
and rubs it with wool till it shines,
then
hangs it up at the threshold,
allowing it to rest
and no more be obliged to strike sparks from the flint.
Human lips
   which have no more to say
keep the shape of the last word spoken
and the hand keeps the feeling of weight
though the pitcher
   lost half its water
      on the way back home.

What now I say is not said by me,
but dug out of the earth, like grains of petrified wheat.
Some
  on coins carve a lion,
others
   a head;
the different coins, the copper, the gold, and the bronze,
honored equally lie in the earth.
The age tried to gnaw them, leaving the print of its teeth.
Time is wearing me down like a coin
and my self is too little for me.

MOSCOW, 1923

Slate Pencil Ode

A mighty meeting—star with star,
the flinty road from the old song,
language of flint and tongue of air,
water with flint, horseshoe, and ring.
On the soft-layered shale of clouds
a slate pencil's milky mark—
not the apprenticeship of worlds,
but sheepish ravings in the dark.

We stand in the dense night asleep,
warmed by this fleecy sheepish cap.
The spring, a warbling chain of speech,
into the mine runs gurgling back.
Here fear and dislocation write
with a white-lead crayon's gleam,
and here a rough draft comes to light
written by scholars of the stream.

Vertiginous cities of goats,
a mighty layering of flints;
and there is yet another ridge—
churches of sheep, their settlements!
The water teaches them, time wears,
the plumb line preaches what they know,
and the transparent woods of air
were sated with them long ago.

Like a dead drone beside the hive
bright day is swept away shamefaced.
And night the predator bears off
the burning chalk to feed the slate.
O, to wipe off the marks of day
from the iconoclastic board
and from the hand shake out the wraith
of visions, like a fledgling bird!

Fruit swelled. The grapes were growing ripe.
Day raged, as day will rage, and soon
came a sweet game of knucklebones
and the fierce collies' furs at noon.
Like garbage from the icy peaks
the hungry water flows and whirls—
the verso of the icons' green—
playing like a puppy with its tail.

And spiderlike it crawls on me,
where every meeting is moon-drenched.
On the astonished craggy steep
against the slate I hear chalk scratch.
Memory, is it you that speaks,
teaching, breaking the night to shards,
flinging chalks where the forest shakes,
tearing them from the beaks of birds?

For us, only the voice explains
all that was scratching, struggling there,
and we shall drag the dusty crayon
where the voice teaches us to steer.
I break the night, the burning chalk,
to trace a firm and short-lived line.
I change the din for arrows' talk,
change symmetry for angry cries.

Who am I? Not a man who builds,
no shipwright and no roofer I—
a double-dealer, double-souled,
champion of daylight, friend of night.
Happy the man who named the flint
a scholar of the flowing stream.
Happy the man who buckled the feet
of mountains on the solid ground.

And now I study the diary
scratched by summer on the slate,
language of flint and tongue of air,
a layering of dark and light,
and I would wish to put my hands
in the flint road of the old song
as in a flesh wound, and so bind
water with flint, horseshoe, and ring.

1923

January 1, 1924

He who has kissed the crown of time's exhausted cranium
will feel a filial tenderness
remembering how time, outside the window,
in a wheat drift lay down to rest.
He who has lifted up his age's sickly eyelids—
two sleepy apples—he will hear
through all eternity the roaring of the rivers
of treacherous and empty years.

The tyrant age has eyes like two great sleepy apples,
a handsome terra-cotta mouth—
but dying, he will fall against the hand of
a son who has said goodbye to youth.
I know, the breath of life, as each day passes, shortens,
and soon now they will put an end
to my song of the wrongs of terra-cotta
and seal my lips with molten tin.

O terra-cotta life! the age's gradual dying!
I fear you will be understood
only by those who wear the helpless smile of people
who have lost themselves in the dark wood.
What agony to seek a word that's vanished,
to lift the patient's lids, and then
with quicklime in the blood, to go by night to gather
herbs for an alien race of men.

Our age ... The quicklime in the son's sick blood grows thicker,
Moscow's asleep, a casket made of wood,
there is no place to run to from our age, the tyrant ...
Snow smells of apples as of old.
I want to run away, to run far from my threshold.
Where shall I hide? The street is dark,
and like the salt they scatter on a cobbled causeway,
my conscience glistens, white on black.

A passenger like most, I've set off on my travels,
in meager furs, not going far,
by alleyways and low-slung eaves and starling houses,
still wrestling to make fast the rug.
A street flicks idly past, and then another,
like apples the sleigh's runners crunch on ice,
the blanket loops put up a stiff resistance
and keep on slipping from my grasp.

Ringing like ironmongery, the night of winter
clatters along the Moscow streets.
A frozen fish, it knocks, and steam comes gushing
from pink cafés, like minnows' silver scales.
Again Moscow is Moscow. I say to her: "Good morning!
Don't lose your mind; all is not lost.
As in the days of old, the brotherhood I honor
of the pike's justice and the frost."

The chemist's raspberry flagon flaming in the snowdrifts;
somewhere the clatter of an Underwood;
the cabbie's back and the deep snow—what more is needed?
You won't be touched. You won't be killed.
Winter-the-beautiful, and stars in the goat heavens
are scattered wide and burn like milk,
and like a horse's tail against the icy runners
the carriage blanket rubs and rings.

But the alleyways were smoking like oil lanterns,
gulping the raspberry ice and snow.
They hear in everything the Soviet sonatina,
remembering 1920. No,
could I surrender to the pillory of slander—
the ice still has an apple smell—
the vow I made the fourth estate, that wonder,
the solemn oath to which we wept?

Who else will you kill now? Who else will you make famous?
What will you make up now, what lies?
Rip out a key from the Underwood's gristly sinew,
you'll find the small bone of the pike.
And in the sick son's blood the quicklime grows and thickens,
and beatific laughter flows ...
but our typewriter's simple sonatinas
are just those great sonatas' ghosts.

1924

*

I shall fling myself through the dark streets' gypsy encampment
in pursuit of a black sprung carriage, a branch of bird cherry,
a hood of snow, and the millrace's din never-ending . . .

I only remember the misfiring of chestnut tresses
smoked over with bitterness, no, with the sharp admixture
of formic acid; they leave on the lips at such moments

the dryness of amber, the atmosphere seems to grow browner,
and rings around the pupils of eyes are arrayed in a lining
of lightness and all that I know of an apple-pink skin . . .

But runners of sleighs on the snow still kept on scraping,
the prickly stars looked down on the wattle of bast-work,
and the hooves of the horse beat time on the frozen piano.

And no light to be seen by the prickly lies of the stars,
and life will float by in the foam of an opera hood,
and no one will say: "From the dark streets' gypsy encampment" . . .

                                                    1925

UNCOLLECTED POEMS (1930–1933)

Leningrad

I've come back to my city, that I know through my tears,
through a child's swollen glands, and deep down in my veins.

You've come back here, then swallow as fast as you can
the fish oil of Leningrad's riverside lamps.

Recognize then, and quickly, December's short days
where black sinister tar with egg yellow is dyed.

Petersburg! I'm not ready to die quite so soon:
You have in your phone book the numbers I know.

Petersburg! I've addresses still fixed in my head
to find all the voices of those who are dead.

On a back stair, a black stair, I live, and the bell,
torn out by the roots, stabs my temple as well,

and I'll wait for those guests, those dear guests, all night long,
while the fetters of door-chains keep singing their song.

DECEMBER 1930

*

With imperial power I was only acquainted in childhood,
being frightened by oysters, but daring to peep at the guardsmen ...
and I owe not a speck of my soul to that obsolete empire,
however I tortured myself to behave like the rest.

With stolid pomposity, scowling from under a beaver,
I never stood guard beneath the Egyptian bank portals,
and never, oh never, by the oily Neva did a gypsy
to the rustle of banknotes come dance her dances for me.

Sensing trouble to come, from the roar of tumultuous action
I fled far away to the Black Sea, among the Nereids,
and from those belles dames—all of them European and tender—
what did I not suffer: embarrassment, injury, grief!

So why then, even today, does that city possess me,
my feelings and thoughts, as if by some ancient commandment,
the place that the fire and the cold have made even more brazen,
so empty, so youthful, self-satisfied, cursed?

Is it because once as a child in a book I caught sight of
good Lady Godiva, her russet hair loosely cascading,
that I'm still repeating these words to myself sotto voce:
farewell then, Godiva ... I do not remember, Godiva ...

JANUARY 1931

48

*

Help me, O Lord, to live through this long night:
I fear for life, I fear for her, your slave—
living in Petersburg's like living in the grave.

JANUARY 1931

*

We'll sit in the kitchen, you and I,
where the white kerosene smells sweet.

A round cob loaf and a sharp knife—
pump up the Primus if you like.

Or gather together bits of string
to tie up the basket before dawn,

so we can go off to the station
where no one will track us down.

LENINGRAD, JANUARY 1931

*

For the noisy valor of future years,
for a lofty race of men,
I have lost my cup at the fathers' feast,
my honor, my cheerfulness.

The wolfhound century leaps on my back,
but I have no wolf in my blood.
O hide me deep and warm, like a cap
in the sleeve of Siberia's coat.

Let me see no coward, no sticky slime,
no wheel with bones and blood,
but silver foxes that shine all night
with a grace from before the flood.

Bear me off to the dark-flowing Yenisey
where pine trees stretch to the moon,
because I have no wolf in my blood,
and shall only be killed by man.

MARCH 17–28, 1931

Batyushkov

Like a flâneur with a magic cane,
tender Batyushkov lives at my place—
wanders down Zamostie lanes,
sniffs a rose, sings Zafna's praise.

Not for a moment believing that we
could be separated, I bowed to him:
I shake his brightly gloved cold hand
in an envious delirium.

He smiled at me. "Thank you," I said,
so shy I could not find the words:
No one commands such curves of sound,
never was there such speech of waves.

With oblique words he made us feel
the wealth and torments that we share—
the buzz of verse-making, brotherhood's bell,
and the harmonies of pouring tears.

And the mourner of Tasso answered me:
"I am not yet used to eulogy;
I only cooled my tongue by chance
on the grape-flesh of poetry."

All right, raise your eyebrows in surprise,
city dweller and city dweller's friend—
like blood samples, from glass to glass
keep pouring your eternal dreams.

JUNE 18, 1932

[Batyushkov: see note on page 15.]

Ariosto

The cleverest man in Italy, untroubled,
suave Ariosto feels a little hoarse.
He revels in his catalogue of fish,
peppers the oceans with malicious babble.

Like a musician playing on ten cymbals,
he tirelessly snaps off the thread of tales,
not knowing his own way, he pulls all ways
his mixed-up story of chivalric scandals.

On the cicada's tongue, a captivating air—
Pushkinian sadness with southern conceit—
he catches Orlando in a web of lies
and shudders, feeling utterly transfixed.

And to the sea he says: Roar without thought.
And to the maiden on the rock: Lie bare ...
Tell us more tales, then, we can't get enough,
as long as blood flows in us and ears hear ...

O town of lizards, where there's not a soul!
If only you could give us more like him,
Callous Ferrara ... Hurry, yet again,
as long as blood flows in us, tell us tales ...

It's cold in Europe, dark in Italy.
Power is repulsive, like a barber's hands.
But he still lords it better, cunningly,
and out through the wide-open window sends

a smile to the hill lambs, and to the monk
on donkey-back, and to the ducal troops,
silly from wine and garlic and the plague,
and to the child that sleeps among blue flies.

But I love his unbridled freedom, love
his foolish language, sweetly salted tongue,
and the enchanting clash of double sounds—
I fear to cut the pearl from the bivalve.

Suave Ariosto, who knows, an age will pass—
and into a single wide fraternal blue
we'll pour your azure and our own black sea.
We too were there. And there we drank the mead.

STARY KRYM, MAY 4–6, 1933

[The last line is a traditional ending for folktales.]

from the VORONEZH NOTEBOOKS (1935–1937)

★

I have to live, though twice now I have died,
and water drives this town out of its mind;

how beautiful it is, cheerful, strong cheekboned, how
sweet is the fat earth's pressure on the plow;

how the spring turns the steppe to its advantage,
and sky, the wide sky, is your Buonarroti.

APRIL 1935

Black Earth

Too black, too much indulged, living in clover,
all little withers, all air, all loving care,
all crumbling, and all massing in a choir—
damp clods of soil, my freedom and my earth!

With early plowing it is black to blueness,
and unarmed labor here is glorified—
a thousand hills plowed open wide to say it—
circumference is not all circumscribed.

And yet the earth is blunder and obtuseness—
no swaying it, even on bended knee:
its rotting flute gives sharpness to the hearing,
its morning clarinet harrows the ear.

How sweet the fat earth's pressure on the plow,
how the spring turns the steppe to its advantage . . .
my greetings then, black earth: be strong, look out—
black eloquence of wordlessness in labor.

APRIL 1935

What's the name of this street?
It's Mandelstam Street.
What a devil of a name!
Turn it this way or that,
it's twisted, not straight.

He wasn't too linear,
no lily, a sinner,
and that's why this street,
or rather, this pit,
is named after that man
called Mandelstam.

APRIL 1935

Children's Haircut

We are still full of life up to the brim,
they still stroll through the cities of the Union,
the blouses and the dresses China-trimmed,
with palmate papilionaceous material.

The number-one clipping machine still grasps
the chestnut-hued backhanders it can get;
and thickly rooted reasonable locks
still flutter to the gleaming serviette.

There are still swifts and swallows in the sky,
no comet has driven us off the rails,
and violet-colored ink sensibly writes
and bears its load of stars and its long tail.

APRIL–MAY 1935

★

Yes, lying in the earth, my lips are moving,
but what I say, each child will learn by heart:

on Red Square the earth is at its roundest,
its voluntary slope more firmly set,

on Red Square the earth is at its roundest,
its slope is unexpectedly unfurled,

dropping away, down to the distant rice fields,
as long as slaves are living in the world.

MAY 1935

The Kama River

I

On this river, the Kama, how dark fills the eyes
when the cities kneel down on the oak of their knees.

Beard to beard, in a gossamer tunic, the firs
look young in the water, they run and they burn.

With a hundred and four sturdy oar blades, the stream
bore us up, bore us down to Kazan and Cherdyn.

There I sailed on the river, the window blind shut,
the window blind shut, and a fire in my head.

And by me my wife didn't sleep for five nights,
didn't sleep for five nights, three guards at her side.

II

Departing, I scanned the coniferous east,
while a buoy took the weight of the Kama in spate.

And I'd love to exfoliate mountains and fire,
but barely have time now to season the firs.

And I'd love to take root, understand if you can,
in the long-standing Urals, long peopled by man.

And I'd love to be able to save and to hold
this insane level space in the tails of my coat.

MAY 1935

[Mandelstam and his wife traveled down the Kama River from Cherdyn to Voronezh.]

★

Robbing me of the seas, a springboard and a sky,
forcing my foot to tread the all-too-solid earth,
what did you gain? With all your strategy
you could not take from me the lips that stir.

MAY 1935

★

A wave runs on, wave breaking a wave's back,
throwing itself at the moon in captive grief,
and janissary-like, the youthful deep,
the unabating capital of waves,
blind, hurls itself to dig a trench in sand.

But through the gloomy flakiness of air
the turrets of an unbuilt wall are glimpsed
and from the foaming stairs fall soldiers
of jealous sultans—torn and dashed to drops—
and the cold eunuchs bring the poison cups.

JULY 1935

*

From past the houses and the trees,
longer than freight trains' harmonies,
hoot while I work and strengthen me,
guardian of gardens and factories.

Hoot, guardian, and sweetly breathe,
like Sadko of Novgorod the free
deep in the seething cobalt sea,
keep hooting through the centuries,
siren of Soviet history.

DECEMBER 6–9, 1936

*

My goldfinch, I'll toss back my head—
let's look at the world, you and I:
a wintry day, prickly as stubble,
is it just as rough on your eye?

Tail like a boat, black and gold plumage,
dipped in paint from the beak down—
are you aware, my little goldfinch,
what a goldfinch dandy you are?

What air there is on his forehead:
black and red, yellow and white!—
he keeps a sharp lookout both ways,
won't look now, he's flown out of sight.

DECEMBER 1936

*

Deep in the hill the idol sits unmoving
in his unbounded, caring, happy chambers,
while from his neck the grease of jewels drips,
protecting dreams that ebb and flow.

When he was a boy, a peacock was his playmate,
they fed him on a rainbow of the Indies
and gave him milk out of rose-colored clay
and never spared the cochineal.

Lulled into sleep the bone is knitted up,
the knees, the hands, the shoulders all made human.
He smiles with his own quietest of smiles,
thinking with bone and feeling with his forehead,
attempting to recall his human features.

DECEMBER 1936

*

Through my cabin windowpane
the distant line of caravans ...
from the frost and from the warmth
the river seems not far away.
And the wood—are those trees pines?

—No, not pines, but lilac lines!—
and that birch tree standing there—
I'll never say just what it is:
just the prose of skylit ink
illegible and light as air ...

DECEMBER 26, 1936

*

Day is a kind of greenhorn now—
I can't make it out—
and the sea barriers stare at me
in anchors and in cloud.

Quiet, quiet on the bleached water
the warships' slow advance,
and the narrow slits of the channels
lie black beneath the ice.

DECEMBER 28, 1936

*

I'll marvel at the world, the snows,
and the children yet a while,
but with a true, authentic as the road,
free, disobedient smile.

DECEMBER 1936

*

Yeast of the world, dear yeast of time—
sounds, and tears, and works of men—
drumbeats like the falling rain
of calamity to come,
sounds that now no longer sound,
out of what ore can they be mined?

In poverty-stricken memory
you first sense blind concavities
filled with water copper-green—
and you walk where they have been,
to your own self unloved, untried—
a blind man and a blind man's guide . . .

JANUARY 12–18, 1937

*

Alone, I look into the frost's face:
nowhere I came from, it is going nowhere,
and still the breathing miracle of the plain
is pleated without a wrinkle, ironed flat.

And in starched poverty the sun
screws up his eyes, tranquil and comforted . . .
The unnumbered forests are still much the same . . .
Eyes crunch the snow, like innocent white bread.

JANUARY 16, 1937

*

What can we do with the deadness of the plains,
the long-drawn hunger of their miracle?
For what we deem to be their openness
we too can see as we drift off to sleep,—
and still the question grows whither and whence
are they? And is he not crawling over them
slowly, the one of whom we cry in sleep,
the Judas of the peoples still to come?

JANUARY 16, 1937

*

I've not died yet, and still I'm not alone
as long as with my poor beloved
I revel in the plains, their cold
magnificence, the mist, the blizzard.

In grand, luxurious poverty
I can live peaceful, live consoled—
blessed be all the days and nights,
blessed the blameless, sweet-voiced toil.

Unhappy the man who like his shadow
fears the barking dogs, the scything wind,
and pitiful who half alive
begs coppers from a shadow's hand.

JANUARY 1937

*

Do not compare: life is incomparable.
I felt a tremor of increasing fear
as I took on the plains' equality
and the wide sky became my malady.

I summoned the air, my servingman,
expecting from him services or news,
made ready to set out, follow the arc
of expeditions that could never start.

Where I have most sky I am glad to roam,
and a clear sadness will not let me leave
Voronezh and its adolescent hills
for the clear human hills of Tuscany.

JANUARY 18, 1937

*

I hear the January ice,
whispering beneath the bridges,
and I remember other skies,
over heads the sharp hops' brightness.

From stale staircases and squares,
palaces all walls and angles,
his lips eaten thin by care,
Dante sang with all the more
power of his Florence circle.

So my shadow feasts its eyes
on that coarse-grained northern granite,
seeing the axman's blocks by night
where the daylight painted mansions,

or my shadow shifts and sighs,
yawns a bit with you from habit,

or it joins the noisy crowd,
seeking warmth in wine or sky,

feeding bread, tasteless and dry,
to the unrelenting swans . . .

JANUARY 22, 1937

*

Like Rembrandt, martyr of the chiaroscuro,
I have gone deep into the days of silence,
but the sharp outline of my burning rib
is not protected by that noble warrior
nor by those guards who sleep beneath the storm.

Can you forgive me, my resplendent brother,
master and father of the black-green shadow?—
but the eye open on the falcon's feather
and the warm caskets of the midnight harem
do not do good, but without goodness trouble
the tribe made restless by the twilight's furs.

FEBRUARY 8, 1937

*

Armed with the eyesight of thin-waisted wasps
that suck at the earth's axis, the earth's axis,
I sense it all, all that I ever saw,
and vainly, word for word, try to recall it . . .

I make no pictures, neither do I sing
nor draw the black-voiced bow across the string:
I only suck on life, and love to envy
the wasps, so potent and so sly.

O if I too could one day be impelled
by summer's heat and by the air's sharp practice
to feel, as I avoided sleep and death,
earth's axis, yes, to penetrate earth's axis . . .

FEBRUARY 8, 1937

*

I sing when my throat is moist and my soul is dry,
and my eyes are damp, and conscience tells no lies.
Is the wine good? And are the fur coats good?
Good the commotion of Colchis in the blood?
The chest is drawn tight, without language, quiet:
and now not I am singing but my breath—
my hearing sheathed in mountains, my head deaf.

A generous song is to itself high praise,
pleasure to friends and pitch to enemies.

A one-eyed song, growing up out of moss,
the one-voiced bounty of the hunter's life,
sung in the saddle or on mountaintops,
holding the breath freely and openly,
with just one honest goal, to bring the bride
and groom to the wedding, safely, angrily . . .

FEBRUARY 8, 1937

★

Rendings of rounded bays, and gravel, and deep blueness,
and the slow sail continuing in cloud,
I have been taken from you, I hardly knew you:
longer than organ fugues, the grass of seas false-haired
is bitter and it smells of lies enduring,
an iron tenderness intoxicates the mind
and rust gnaws weakly at the sloping shoreline . . . Why then
do I feel underneath my head a different sand?
You, Ural of the throat, the Volga lands' broad shoulders,
or this flat territory—these are my only rights,
and I must breathe them in to fill my lungs.

FEBRUARY 8, 1937

*

O how I wish that I
unnoticed and untraced
could fly after the light
where the I is quite lost.

And you, shine in that ring—
no happiness but that—
as from the stars you learn
the meaning of that light.

But what I am whispering here
I want to say to you,
that with this whisper I
give you, child, to the light.

It is only a gleam
and it is only light
when whispering gives it power
and lisping is delight.

MARCH 27, 1937

*

The potters exalt the blue island—
Crete the gay, their gift is baked in
the echoing earth. Hear the thrashing
of the dolphins' underground fins.

This sea is there for the taking
in the clay made glad by the glaze,
and the ice-cold strength of the vessel
is split between sea and eyes.

Give me back what is mine, blue island,
winged Crete, give me back my task,
and nourish the glazed earthen vessel
at the goddess's flowing breast.

This is and was sung, and was blue
long before Odysseus came,
before the time when the food
and drink were called "mine" and "thine."

Grow well again, radiate,
star of the ox-eyed sky,
and the flying fish is just chance,
and the water that answers "Aye."

MARCH 1937

*

There are women who are akin to the damp earth
and their every step is a deeply echoed sobbing,
their calling is to accompany the risen,
to be the first to welcome the newly dead,
and to ask them for tenderness is a kind of crime,
and to take leave of them is impossible.
Today—an angel, tomorrow—a graveyard worm,
and the following day—no more than a shady outline.
What was once a step will be inaccessible . . .
Everlasting the flowers. The sky incorruptible,
and all that is still to come is just a promise.

MAY 4, 1937